Ebenezer Howard
An illustrated life of
Sir Ebenezer Howard
1850-1928
John Moss-Eccardt

Contents

Opposite: Sir Ebenezer Howard OBE JP, in his seventies.

Cover image courtesy of First Garden City Heritage Museum, Letchworth.

ACKNOWLEDGEMENTS
The author and publishers wish to thank the following for permission to reproduce the illustrations on the pages indicated: Letchworth Museum First Garden City Collection, 2, 9, 11, 13, 17 (top and bottom), 18, 26, 27, 29 (top and bottom), 32, 35 (top and bottom), 36, 40, 43, 47; Guildhall Library, 4; Welwyn Garden City Library 38, 39, 41 (top and bottom), 44.

Copyright © 1973 by John Moss-Eccardt. First published June 1973.
Transferred to digital print on demand 2011. ISBN 978 0 74781 131 2.

Printed in Great Britain by PrintOnDemand-Worldwide.com, Peterborough, UK.

Fore Street, London EC2, the street where Howard was born.
A commemorative plaque is affixed to Moor House, London Wall.

The preparation

Ebenezer Howard was born on 29th January 1850, within the sound of Bow bells, at 62 Fore Street in the City of London. His father, Ebenezer, was a baker and confectioner from Harwich; his mother Ann was a farmer's daughter from Lincolnshire. The exact details of the Howard business are difficult to determine as accounts of it differ, but it is certain that at the time of Ebenezer's birth the family was able to live in modest comfort and security. Four of the nine Howard children died in infancy, Ebenezer being the eldest surviving son; he had two elder sisters, Elizabeth and Anne.

Ebenezer senior was a healthy, energetic and hard-working man whose day's labour began at 3.00 a.m. and lasted into the evening. His vitality was matched by a strong constitution and it was his proud boast that he had never suffered from a headache in over seventy years. Like most of his contemporaries in trade, he believed in the dignity of labour and a man's ability to make his way in life through a combination of integrity and a practised intelligence. His failure as a businessman was due to his compassion for his fellow men and an absent-mindedness for which he was notorious. He was upright, sincere, a humanitarian, and well loved by all. Even when bankrupt he did not press for money owed to him and he never allowed business worries to disturb the tranquillity of his home. His wife had the common sense of her country origin and was able to share in the management of the business to good effect. Thus the very earliest influences in the young Ebenezer's life were based on the affection, industry and security provided by both parents.

SCHOOLDAYS
Because of his mother's preoccupation with the shop and with the younger children, Ebenezer went away to school at the age of four. Such separations were quite frequent until

relatively recent times and writers about Howard seem to have ignored the effect that leaving home at such an early age might have had on him. Suffice it to say that certain contradictory traits of his character could possibly have originated at this point in his life; the family life of Fore Street was now replaced by the communal life of a school at Sudbury, Suffolk. He remained there in the care of two maiden ladies until the age of nine: he acquired a taste for poetry and considered himself to have been well taught. His next school, at Cheshunt, brought him into contact for the first time with the Hertfordshire countryside. The school grounds were spacious and pleasant but Ebenezer made slow progress in his studies. He returned to Suffolk at the age of twelve, attending Stoke Hall, Ipswich, where he continued his unremarkable academic career until he was fifteen years old.

There are unmistakable signs of an inclination towards practical matters in this youthful period. Drawing and maps interested him at school, while his hobbies included swimming, cricket, stamp collecting and photography. His reading appears to have been limited to the *Boys' Own Magazine,* his interest in the arts to a single visit to the Alhambra theatre at the age of eighteen. During the time he spent at home he sought the company of his father rather than his mother and attended the Poultry Chapel with him. Father and son, as Congregationalists, tended to combine in criticism of Mrs Howard's Calvinist creed; it is no wonder that in later years Ebenezer took a keen interest in religious matters.

EARLY CAREER

It was quite natural that Ebenezer's father should find him a place in a City office in which to begin his working career and in 1865 he entered the office of Messrs Greaves and Son, stockbrokers, of Warnford Court, London. His duties were mainly to copy out letters into a book using a quill pen, his reward a glass of wine at the end of the day. He next became a junior clerk to Mr C. Elliot, merchant, and remained there some three years. During this period he taught himself Pitman's shorthand, an accomplishment which played a major part in the development of his early career. He then exchanged commerce for the law and worked in solicitors' offices, first with E. Kimber of Winchester Buildings, and then Messrs Pawle, Livesey and Fearon whose offices were near Temple Bar.

The Sunday visits to the Poultry Chapel had an interesting outcome, for there Ebenezer met Dr Joseph Parker. Dr Parker was famous as a preacher and later became Minister of the City Temple. One Sunday Ebenezer took down Parker's sermon in shorthand and sent him the result. He invited the young scribe to call on him and gave him the job of private secretary. This post lasted for three months until, as Howard says, 'he got tired of paying my wages'. He seemed to have impressed the reverend gentleman who told him that he should have been a preacher. That he influenced the young man is beyond doubt; the very work Ebenezer did would have been full of the preacher's rolling phrases, while his enthusiasm and drive must have given him his first experience of a man of more than ordinary stature. Here was a thinker whose mind ranged widely over a variety of subjects, yet kept matters within disciplined and practical bounds. This became Ebenezer Howard's own approach to such questions as interested him. It seems likely that his acquaintance with Dr Parker made him realise that he was dissatisfied with his somewhat limited way of life, and prompted his next step.

A NEW WORLD

At the age of twenty-one, the combination of ambition and a suspected weakness of the lungs sent Ebenezer to America, the land of opportunity. A farmer uncle had given him the idea of making a living from the soil and so, in 1871, he and two friends sailed for the New World.

On arrival in New York they set out for Iowa and while there heard of farming land to be had in Howard County, Nebraska. They each took up 160 acres of state land, built a shanty for sleeping and began the new life. Howard planted maize, potatoes, water-melons, and cucumbers; the latter was his only successful crop and he became a hired hand to the one successful farmer in the trio. At this time he was also preaching in a small church which he helped to form called, strangely enough, the Ebenezer Church: this activity would, no doubt, have pleased Dr Parker!

In 1872 Ebenezer Howard and one friend moved to Chicago where Ebenezer was able to find work. In the firm of Ely, Burnham and Bartlett of 206 La Salle began a career which was to provide his main income for the greater part of his life. His youthful efforts to master Pitman's shorthand now bore fruit giving him, as a stenographer, entry to those places where business, administration and the law were practised, and allowing him an insight into aspects of public affairs which were to be of use to him in his future work of exposition and persuasion. His note-taking was at the rate of 250 words per minute and there is little doubt that the ability to concentrate, and think clearly, which he showed all his life was greatly developed by the practice of this profession.

From his lodgings at 374 Michigan Avenue, Ebenezer sallied forth to work, to fish in the river Calumet, to visit the theatre, or the Congregational Church. Howard himself claimed that his stay in Chicago had a great influence on his life, giving him a fuller and wider outlook on religious and social questions than he would have gained in England. His circle of friends included Alonzo M. Griffin, another shorthand writer, with whom he discussed matters of religion. These two friends were commissioned by the *Chicago Times* to report verbatim an address by Mrs Cora Richmond, a well-known trance speaker. Howard was very impressed by her and became interested in spiritualism; he visited her on several occasions and it is alleged that she made some forecast of his future involvement with matters touching the benefit of humanity. Some time later he read Tom Paine's *Age of Reason* which seems to have loosened his bonds of orthodoxy, making him what he chose to call a 'freethinker'. He retained throughout his life a strange blend of all his religious traits which often showed themselves in his mode of expression.

This intellectual development was tempered with an intense interest in practical matters. The conversion of a conventional pocket watch into a keyless model, and a single-shot gun into a repeater began a preoccupation with mechanical inventions which became a dominating element in his life. It may be that the mechanisms of firearms brought him into contact with the firm of E. Remington and Sons, the small arms manufacturers of Ilion, New York, who from 1847 manufactured the Scholes and Slidden typewriter, later to become the Remington Model 1. Certainly he became interested in the problems of alignment and differential spacing, and made several trips to New York between 1876 and 1879 in connection with the firm: he also

Ebenezer Howard in his mid thirties.

seems to have been involved in the introduction of these machines to the Continent with his brother-in-law, John Harrison. His connection with typewriters led to his lifelong efforts to perfect a shorthand machine.

THE SEED SOWN?

Probably the most important and, perhaps, controversial aspect of his stay in the United States concerns the way in which his garden city ideas came to be formed. Several writers have been a little surprised at Howard's denials of having been influenced towards those ideas while living there: he claimed that he was at that time too preoccupied with religious matters. Whatever the case may be, there are several interesting common factors in the Chicago scene of that time and the garden city idea which he eventually put forward. The first of these was the relationship between the production of foodstuffs and their eventual marketing in the towns. Howard must have become aware of the waste of time and money involved in getting agricultural produce to the city markets; he must also have recognised the need for efficiency in farming, and the importance of mechanisation was brought home to him during his brief career as a farmer.

The tremendous expansion of Chicago from 12,000 to 307,000 inhabitants between 1845 and 1870, and the accompanying rocketing of land prices must have made some impression on him too. It seems equally likely that the fact that Chicago was known as 'The Garden City' before its disastrous fire on 8th October 1871, was brought to his notice. Finally, at a distance of some four miles west of Chicago's limits lay a town called Riverside where an interesting experiment was under way. Planned by Frederick Law Olmsted, this town had 700 of its 16,000 acres devoted to green roads, borders, parks and other features which produced a pleasing blend of town and country. Within this environment the Riverside citizen could pursue rural activities in congenial surroundings which combined the benefits of both worlds. Did not this idyllic scene cause some stirrings in the mind of the founder of the first garden city?

THE RETURN AND MARRIAGE

The young man who returned to England in 1876 was very different from the one who had set out four years before at the age of twenty-one. These years had been filled with new experiences and impressions which had contributed greatly to the development of his ideas and his personality. As an experienced stenographer of considerable ability he was able to join the firm of Gurney's, official reporters to Parliament; at this time he was living with his parents at Stoke Newington. Within two years he had entered partnership with a Mr Treadwell, also a stenographer; but because he was treated badly by his senior partner Howard terminated the relationship. This brief venture was his only attempt at running a business on his own behalf; from then on he worked from an office at 11 New Court, Carey Street, both as stenographer and garden city propagandist.

There is very little information on Howard's relations with the opposite sex. That he was familiar with a feminine environment follows from the number of his female relations and the close-knit family relationship which existed between them. At eighteen, during a visit to the Alhambra theatre, the

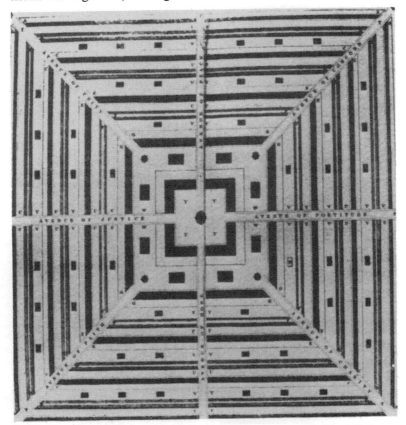

The plan of Buckingham's model town of Victoria from 'National Evils and Practical Remedies', 1849. This should be compared with Howard's diagram 'Garden City and Rural Belt'.

predicament of a 'rather modest' girl on the stage prompted in him the romantic notion of rescuing her; fortunately, it remained a notion! In Chicago he belonged to the Order of the Golden Fleece whose members were bound to escort a lady to the Congregational Church each Sunday; the selection of the lady was made by the Church and the escort was notified by letter. Howard's contact with ladies must have gone beyond the mere carrying out of his escort duties, for he became engaged to a Miss Kelhuiston, a sister of a friend of his, but unfortunately she died soon after his return to England.

Ebenezer's next attachment was to prove considerably more fortunate and in 1879 he married Elizabeth Ann Bills of Nuneaton. Charming, with presence and a sense of humour, she was an important influence in his life and a firm believer in his work; she was an ideal wife for him. They had four children, Cecil, Edith, Kathleen, and Margery; their home life was very happy and Mrs Howard managed the family finances expertly. This was very necessary as her husband easily parted with money for some public cause or for the development of one of his numerous, but never lucrative, mechanical inventions. The couple were never irritable or annoyed with the children and the shortage of money seems to have made no difference at all to their enjoyment of life. The children did notice, however, that their father was inclined to become absorbed in his own thoughts or activities. Even during one of his relaxations, watching cricket at the Oval, he would become oblivious of the presence of his offspring if he had taken one of them there with him. During this period he went to America again, once or twice, in connection with the Remington typewriter.

THE METHOD

It has often been said that Howard *invented* garden cities and attention has been drawn to the similarity between the methods of the inventor of mechanical devices and the way in which the garden city idea came about. There can be no disagreement concerning the pre-eminently practical approach which he adopted towards the problems which interested him. Coupled with this was an apparent lack of self-interest which enabled him to see his objectives clearly and uncluttered by the impaired judgement that self-seeking produces.

Living in an age where social stratigraphy was more rigid than

The first Mrs Howard a year before her death. Howard owed much to her support and encouragement.

in our own, he seems to have been untroubled by social pretensions or aspirations, being more concerned with the lot of the less fortunate than for himself. This attitude must surely have stemmed from his religious convictions which were strong but not sectarian, his liberal political views, and an idealism strongly tinged with a pinch of scepticism. His own view was: 'I am, indeed, as my friends know, a man of some faith; but I am also—perhaps the combination is somewhat rare—a terrible sceptic.' Finally, we might add the lack of a sophisticated higher education to the advantages enjoyed by this observer of the chaos and squalor of late nineteenth-century industrial England. In contrast, many of his contemporaries had allowed their minds to become filled to bursting with the copious outpourings of the reformers of this and previous centuries.

Through his church connections and his professional contacts Howard became conversant with leading questions of the day and their protagonists. Subjects ranged over religion and science, politics, poverty and riches, economics, urban congestion, and the decline of the countryside. He became involved in discussions on these topics but was especially interested in questions of social significance. He went to the heart of the matter when he wrote in his book: 'Religious and political questions too often divide us into hostile camps; and so in the very realms where calm, dispassionate thought and pure emotions are the essentials of all advance towards right beliefs and sound principles of action, the din of battle and the struggles of contending hosts are more forcibly suggested to the onlooker than the really sincere love of truth and love of country which, one may yet be sure, animate nearly all breasts.'

By temperament Ebenezer Howard was as capable of championing a cause as those with whom he debated but he was able to stand a little apart and assess the value of what he had learnt, just as the inventor must prove his various modifications before adapting them. Thus, little by little, a recipe was concocted from the various ideas which he heard and tested against his common sense. One may imagine him like a small boat steering his way through the shoals of opinions always holding to his course until he reaches harbour.

In 1888 Edward Bellamy wrote a book which was published in the United States and was to have a great influence in Howard's life. A friend sent him a copy, knowing the Englishman's interest in such matters. *Looking Backward* was just the catalyst needed to make Howard's fermenting mixture of reforming zeal and practicality react most strongly. In later years he describes his introduction to the book. 'This I read at a sitting, not at all critically, and was fairly carried away by the eloquence and evidently strong convictions of the author. This book graphically pictured the whole American nation organised on co-operative principles—this mighty change coming about with marvellous celerity—the necessary mental and ethical changes having previously occurred with equal rapidity. The next morning as I went up to the City from Stamford Hill I realised, as never before, the splendid possibilities of a new civilisation based on service to the community and not on self-interest, at present the dominant motive. Then I determined to take such part as I could, however small it might be, in helping to bring a new civilisation into being.' His first act was to get the book published in Britain by offering to dispose of a hundred copies himself. He discussed Bellamy's ideas with his friends and 'was led to put forward proposals for testing out Bellamy's principles though on a very much smaller scale—in brief, to build by private enterprise pervaded by public spirit an entirely new town, industrial, residential, and agricultural.'

The path signposted

It becomes clear immediately that Bellamy's idea of a communistic Boston of A.D.2000 did not recommend itself to this more liberal critic who distrusted a scheme based on state initiative and preferred a voluntary co-operative organisation. Continual thought and discussion eventually produced the kind of solution he sought. Agricultural land was to be let to various tenants, securing the increment of land values for the benefit of the townspeople; he proposed the same for industries. From this basis began the gestation of *Tomorrow* and for the next ten years he devoted himself to producing the blueprint of his 'path to peaceful reform'. The work was done at odd times gleaned from the hours spent in the very necessary business of making a living. He wrote on the dining table, often during meals, at Kyverdale Road, Stoke Newington, and copies were typed by a cousin because he couldn't afford to pay a professional typist. As the work grew he circulated the typescript to friends both in local government and in the church. In spite of great interest in his ideas from various sections of his circle, the book remained in typescript form as no one would risk its publication; but fate seemed to take a hand when help came from a friend known to Howard and his wife through a common interest in religion.

In a letter to J.W. Cole written in 1927 Howard describes how the unexpected kindness of this friend expedited the publication of *Tomorrow*. 'My wife and I were very close friends of Mr and Mrs George Dickman, and on a visit to them by my wife, shortly before his death, George Dickman said to her, "How is Ben getting on with his book about his proposed garden cities?" My wife told him the manuscript had been completed but there was much difficulty about getting it published. Thereupon George said "Tell Ben if £50 is any use to him he can have it, either as a loan, or as a gift." This enabled me to have the book printed and it was published towards the end of 1898 by Swan Sonnenschein, under the title *Tomorrow.*'

Tomorrow: A Peaceful Path to Real Reform was published in October 1898 and was received favourably. *The Times* commented: 'The only difficulty is to create such a City, but that is a small matter to Utopians.' The *Fabian News* was not so tolerant: 'His plans would have been in time if they had been submitted to the Romans when they conquered Britain. They set about laying out cities, and our forefathers have dwelt in them to this day. Now Mr Howard proposes to pull them down and substitute garden cities, each duly built according to pretty coloured plans, nicely designed with a ruler and compass. The author has read many learned and interesting writers, and the extracts he makes from their books are like plums in the unpalatable dough of his Utopian scheming. We have got to make the best of our existing cities, and proposals for building new ones are about as useful as would be arrangements for protection against visits from Mr Wells's Martians.' Of the book Howard says '. . . my friends and supporters never regarded this book, any more than I did, as more than a sketch or outline of what we hoped to accomplish.'

The Fabian comment was more than unkind: it was unfair and showed a complete inability to understand the plan. The book was the mere beginning of a campaign and a practical means of working out his ideas. For mechanical working parts he substituted words and from these emerged a scheme as real as any of his mechanical concepts. Before the book appeared many people were already won over to the garden city idea and after publication Howard and his followers embarked on a series of lectures to further his project, for it was his aim to bring a garden city into being. It must be admitted, however, that the book did not become a best-seller, nor did its author receive any recognition by those who specialised in political, economic or sociological matters. Those very factors which enabled him to see clearly with eyes unbiased by preconceptions, in particular his lack of academic background, kept him out of the charmed circle of the Establishment. Once the garden city became a physical reality, it could not be ignored—it was a social phenomenon.

Tomorrow represents the culmination of a century-long preoccupation with the consequences of the Industrial

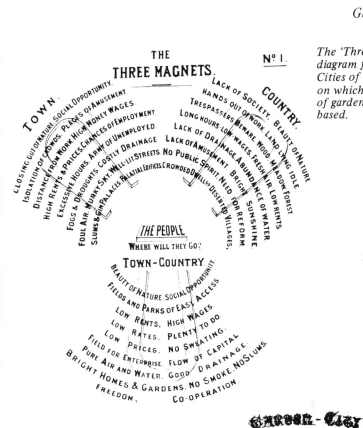

The 'Three Magnets'
diagram from 'Garden
Cities of Tomorrow'
on which the principle
of garden cities was
based.

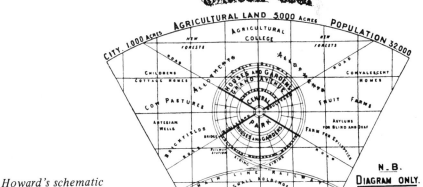

Howard's schematic
diagram for a garden city from
'Garden Cities of Tomorrow':
Notice the author's statement
on its diagrammatic nature.

GARDEN CITY AND RURAL BELT

17

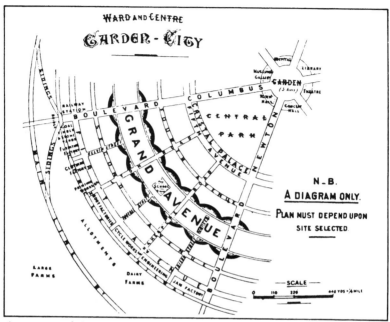

A segment of the central town arrangement from 'Garden Cities of Tomorrow'. This illustrates an inventor's love of detail and respect for practical men.

Revolution. With a few exceptions like Port Sunlight and Bournville, the majority of contributions were theoretical, often verging on the philosophical, and aimed at ideal communities which were never expected to come into being. They intended in the main to influence the social conscience of society and their schemes were often conceived without taking economic considerations into account. There is little evidence to show that Howard had read at all widely in the literature of sociology and one is forced to the conclusion that the garden city concept was the fruit of a remarkable and logical intellect seasoned with an even greater intuition. His ability to go straight to the kernel of a matter is illustrated by statements of social realism such as the following. 'Probably the chief cause of failure in former social experiments has been a misconception of the principal element in the problem—human nature itself. The degree of strain which average human nature will bear in an altruistic direction has not been duly considered by those who have essayed the task of suggesting new forms of social organisations.' Starting, therefore, with an assumption that the problem of overcrowded cities could be solved he began an exposition of this solution, including considerable financial detail, in a book written in a clear, realistic, enthusiastic and competent style.

THE BLUEPRINT

In characteristic fashion the book begins with a number of quotations designed to show that the problem of overcrowded cities and a depopulated countryside was very much in the minds of leading figures of the day. Having thus stated the problem, its nature is examined, and from this emerges the fundamental concept of the 'magnet', an inventor's touch, no doubt! Those features of cities which caused people to live in them, in preference to the country, he termed 'attractions' and likened this 'attraction' to the power of a magnet. The power of the town magnet is greater than that of the country magnet and the only means of solving the problem is to combine the attractions of both in the town-country magnet. 'Town and country must be married,' he declared, 'and out of this joyous union will spring a new hope, a new life, a new civilisation.'

The members of the projected community would, in part, be provided by an organised but voluntary movement of town-dwellers into the country; Professor Alfred Marshall had first proposed this in an article in 1884. The suggestion was that committees and employers should induce workmen to migrate and form industrial colonies in the country where work and housing would be available for them. Howard was able to think beyond this; he saw that the migration of a large group of people to a country area would cause the value of that land to rise, just as it had done during his time in the United States. This increase in value was to be secured to the people who had caused it, once the various initial commitments had been met. The estate was to consist of 6,000 acres of agricultural land which was to be purchased for £240,000 raised on mortgage debentures. The management of the estate was to be in the hands of trustees who were to hold the land for the debenture holders and for the inhabitants. The ground rents which were to be based on the annual value of the land were to be received by the trustees who would pay for items such as interest, and a sinking fund, devoting the remainder to the maintenance of services and similar matters. In addition, after redemption of debentures, the revenue should provide a surplus which could be used for special purposes. The calculations produced by the author show that in a population of 32,000 persons, a rent-rate of £2 per head would produce an income of £54,400 *per annum.*

For the agriculturalist there were benefits as Howard must have realised from his own experience as a farmer. The garden city would provide a ready market of 30,000 souls almost on the doorstep, keeping transport costs to an absolute minimum, offering a steady demand for fruit and vegetables, and cutting out the necessity for the middle man. An efficient sewerage disposal system would provide a steady supply of fertilizer for the soil. Remembering that the revenue from tenants was to be paid to the community, and that this was to go to public services and other community projects, it can be seen that the farmer could enjoy advantages beyond those of mere profit as a return for his participation in the garden city. The estimated revenue from the agricultural part of the estate was £9,750.

The 'town estate' or non-agricultural area was to consist of one thousand acres which cost £40,000. To recover sufficient to pay the interest on the purchase of the land it would be necessary to levy a mere 1s 1d per annum per head of a 30,000 population. Additional money would be needed to supply services and benefits. What the community obtained in exchange for this sum was set out in some detail; these were sites for homes averaging 20 feet by 130 feet; magnificent roads, wide and spacious with abundant trees, shrubs and grass to provide a semi-rural appearance. Other ample sites were to be provided for town hall, public library, museum and picture gallery, theatre, concert hall, hospital, schools, churches, swimming-baths, public markets etc. There was to be a central park of 145 acres, with an avenue 420 feet wide, extending in a circle of over three miles. A railway 4½ miles long would encompass the town. Warehouses, factories, markets, and a centre devoted to shopping were to occupy 82 acres. It is important to note that what might be thought of as ingredients of yet another Utopia is a perfectly workable fiscal scheme.

FINANCIAL SCHEME

The overall calculations, although to modern eyes totally

meaningless in terms of the sums involved, are interesting indications of Howard's working method of building up his scheme on a system which could be implemented by the mere substitution of actual figures for hypothetical averages. The basis for the revenue is explained in the book but the figures merit inclusion here. The gross revenue of the entire estate was to be:

Rate-rent from agricultural estate	£9,750
Rate-rent from 5,500 home building lots at £6 per lot	£33,000
Rate-rent from business premises	£21,250
	£64,000

This sum would be disposed of as follows:

For interest on purchase money £240,000 @ 4%	£9,600
For sinking fund (30 years)	£4,400
For such purposes as are defrayed out of the rates in local authorities	£50,000
	£64,000

There now follows a more detailed examination of the expenditure on services and a comparison between costs of these in London and in the garden city. A final short summary shows why the revenue of a garden city should yield better results than that of other towns. Among the factors given are: low expenditure on the purchase of existing buildings and the payment of compensation for disturbance; few legal costs in connection with previous buildings; great saving in the cost of works because of careful planning of development; the use of labour-saving machinery in areas where it would not be hindered by existing structures. A further chapter goes into more details of expenditure including the matter of security for the debenture holders, and rates levied by 'local bodies within whose jurisdiction the estate is situated.'

ADMINISTRATION AND SERVICES
Having provided a sound financial foundation for the garden city, Howard turns to a discussion of the division to be made between town enterprise and private enterprise in the provision

of services. He seemed inclined more toward a local authority arrangement but felt that public services should justify their continued existence by their efficiency, not being granted a monopoly as in the case of other social experiments. The construction of houses, shops, workshops and factories was to be carried out by individuals or co-operative organisations; no provision had been made in the capital available for such purposes.

His administrative system was to consist of a Central Council and a number of departments. The Central Council would have greater powers of control over its affairs than any other municipal body because as landlords they were at liberty to do what they liked with their land and revenue without the restrictions imposed by acts of Parliament. The powers of the council were to be delegated to the departments which roughly covered the activities undertaken by local authorities today. The members of the Central Council were to be elected by the usual democratic processes, their fitness to serve being estimated by their fellow citizens.

Markets were an important feature of the garden city and here a plan known as 'local option' was to operate. This was designed to limit the number of shops selling a particular type of merchandise while at the same time encouraging the shopkeepers to provide good service and reasonable prices. Should their methods and goods not please the customers, the town administration would set up another trader in the same line of business. Such traders were thus dependent on the goodwill of their customers which they could build up and retain if they managed their affairs wisely and well. Their status became close to that of municipal employees and the working conditions offered their employees would also be a matter of interest to the community.

Local option was to be exercised with regard to public houses also; the community would see that public houses did not increase in numbers beyond necessity. Howard did not wish to prohibit alcohol or public houses, and he was aware that if alcohol were prohibited it would increase traffic in it as had been the case in the United States.

Howard did not forget the situation of the working people who were to live in the garden city. Lacking the necessary capital for the purchase of a house, they would need a source of finance for home-building. The garden city was to encourage building societies, co-operative societies, friendly societies and trade unions to provide loans for this purpose. In a chapter called 'Some Difficulties Considered', he provides something of a mixed bag, covering the matter of personal freedom and communism, discovery and invention, human failing and selfishness as a hindrance to the success of social experiments, and, finally, the great advantages offered by the garden city as compared with other schemes.

After drawing attention to the schemes which are combined in his own ideas, Howard summarises his proposals and says wisely, 'that the mind of the public should not be confused, or the efforts of organisers wasted in a premature attempt to accomplish this work on a national scale, but the great thought and attention shall be first concentrated on a single movement yet one sufficiently large to be at once attractive and resourceful.' Three further chapters are concerned with the effect of garden cities on society, how the system can be integrated into industrial life, and how 'satellite towns' will make it possible for cities to grow without producing urban overcrowding which the garden city concept seeks to cure. Finally, the thorny subject of London is tackled bringing Howard's cycle of thought back to its starting point.

THE PLANNING

Almost the entire book is devoted to the means by which the garden city should be begun and maintained and only a fraction touches on its layout. Unlike the Utopians, Howard did not waste time and energy in working out details of the outward form of the city but concentrated on the processes which would make it possible; he saw clearly that true planning of such a town would have to be done by specialists. It is surprising to find that, even today, many people associate Ebenezer Howard with town planning in spite of the fact that the subject is hardly mentioned in his book and that he provides no plans, but merely sketches and diagrams. Of course there were certain dispositions that he wished to make within the framework of the estate and he specifies that one sixth of it, 1,000 acres, should be devoted to the city proper. The Model Town of Victoria was conceived by J.S. Buckingham as a series of squares placed one within the other while six avenues radiated from a central square. Ebenezer Howard arranged his town on a series of concentric circles with six radiating boulevards and a central park. The similarity between the two cannot be very significant, since it would be very difficult for any two designers using geometric figures not to produce elements of each other's work, particularly when needing roads for access to the centre.

The most interesting aspect of the Howard diagrams is the arrangement of the area into zones for various activities. By doing this the cities were spared the disturbance, noise and pollution of industry while allowing it to be sited within the town limits. The outer ring of the town was, therefore, to comprise workshops, factories and warehouses which would be served by the circular railway system. The Crystal Palace, a glass arcade occupying the fifth circle next to the Central Park, was to be the main marketing area for manufactured goods while the central circular area was to be 5½ acres of well laid-out gardens surrounded by the main public buildings. The third circle was to be occupied by the Grand Avenue of houses and gardens, schools, and places of worship; the houses were to be grouped in crescentic form. The building lots were to measure 20 feet by 130 feet; the buildings were to be varied in design but in harmony with the overall scheme. It can be seen here that even in a formal matter of a diagram, the designer's liberal views shine through his arrangements to ensure the maximum freedom of choice for his garden citizens.

This, then, was stage one of Howard's campaign completed. The book served him as a personal testing ground for his ideas and a means of winning supporters for the garden city project. In it he showed that he was no crank but the exponent of a sensible scheme, which, if properly understood, would make a great contribution to solving the major problems brought about by urban overcrowding. At the same time he also sought to provide those things for his citizens which would contribute to their health and happiness. It now remained to get the project started: 'One small Garden City must be built as a working model, and then a group of cities ... These tasks done, and done well, the reconstruction of London must inevitably follow ...'

Achievement

On 10th June 1899 the Garden City Association was formed 'promoting in its main features, by educational and other means, the project suggested by Mr Ebenezer Howard in his book *Tomorrow: a Peaceful Path to Real Reform'*. Meetings were held, lectures given and pamphlets published. There is a reassuring consistency about the way in which proposals in the book were carried out where possible and principles adhered to; such features must have inspired confidence. For example, Howard repeatedly explains that details are provided merely to give his scheme some real substance; this is borne out in a published outline by the Association which 'is not committed to any of Mr Howard's suggestions with regard to details, its object being to carry out the general principles advocated by him with the assistance of the best available practical advice and assistance.' The practical advice and assistance became available and many able men from business and the professions became members of the Association. So successful was the Association in its work that it enthusiastically resolved to form a limited company called Garden City Limited with a share capital of £50,000 as early as May 1900 but nothing came of the resolution. In 1901 Ralph Neville KC became chairman and Thomas Adams the Association's paid secretary. A conference was held at Bournville which three hundred delegates attended; in the following year at Port Sunlight this number increased to one thousand. Membership of the Association included an impressive number of influential public figures and in June 1902 decisive action was agreed on at a meeting in the Crown Room, Holborn Restaurant, with Earl Grey in the Chair.

PIONEERING VENTURES

As a result of the June meeting, the Garden City Pioneer Company was registered with a capital of £20,000. Its objects

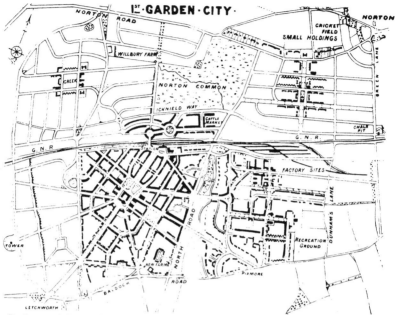

Parker and Unwin's plan for the First Garden City, 1903. Although only a preliminary plan, it was little changed in execution.

were the implementation of Howard's book, now reissued as *Garden Cities of Tomorrow*. Ralph Neville was chairman and the directors were Edward Cadbury, Ebenezer Howard, T.H.W. Idris, H.D. Pearsall, Franklin Thomasson, T.P. Ritsema and Aneurin Williams. Within four months of the issue of the prospectus, the capital was fully subscribed. Hectic activity followed and suitable sites were sought while the winning of support continued all over the country.

Mrs Howard helped and encouraged her husband in spreading the gospel of the garden city idea. The success she enjoyed in this work is shown in an incident related by her husband in a letter which appears in Macfadyen's *Sir Ebenezer Howard*. 'About ten years ago (*c.* 1899) my late wife was speaking to a meeting of working women not far from your house—at Tottenham. We were even then forming a Garden City Association—just a body to talk and write about the subject and to stir the minds of men and women to its possibilities. No Garden City was then in existence; and no money to build it

The Mrs Howard Memorial Hall designed by Parker and Unwin, meeting place of the Letchworth community for many years.

either; and no people of "influence" connected with the movement. But what we needed was a little money for propaganda work. Well, my wife, as I say, was speaking, and after she sat down, fourteen working women each paid 1s and became members of the Garden City Association. And one of them said to her, "We do not expect the Garden City you have talked about to come in our lifetime; but if it comes in our children's and our grandchildren's lifetime our shillings will have been well spent." ' He goes on to remark that the Garden City is a 'practical gospel for working people—aye and for all people.' One can well imagine what inroads all this activity made on the amount of time given up to the practice of stenography and the earning of daily bread. The long-suffering Mrs Howard once wrote in a letter to her husband: 'I could wish that the good Lord who made you a Social Reformer had also given you the wherewithal to reform on.'

The Association organised lectures on 'garden cities as a solution of the housing problem' which were addressed 'to educational, social, political, co-operative, municipal, religious and temperance societies and institutions'. From 17th August 1902 to 17th May 1903 the Association offered over 260 meetings or lectures illustrated by 'limelight views' in locations ranging from Cheapside to Edinburgh. Howard's name appears on the list of lecturers sixteen times. These appearances did not include his attendance at conferences, executive and site meetings, or business appointments. He was now a 'public figure' and as such was often an object of surprise to those who did not know him. He was mild, unassuming, and unconcerned with his personal appearance. In later years Shaw described him as 'this amazing man' who seemed 'an elderly nobody'. There were, however, signs of sterling quality in his personality, particularly as transmitted through his speaking voice. He was naturally eloquent, and public speaking gave him the same kind of stimulus that many people get from outdoor pursuits and sports. On the platform he could hold and persuade his audience, yet in private or business relationships he was not impressive. It seems as if he could only use his personality to the full when faced with the stimulus of an audience or, perhaps, a challenge.

REALISATION

In 1903 a suitable site was chosen at Letchworth near Hitchin in Hertfordshire where 3,818 acres were purchased for £155,587 or £40 15s per acre. On 1st September 1903 the First Garden City Limited was registered with an authorised capital of £300,000. A thousand shareholders and guests attended the formal opening of the First Garden City at Letchworth on 9th October; Earl Grey presided over the proceedings. By this time the Garden City Association had 2,500 members, and Ebenezer Howard, at the age of 53 years, was able to see his concept close to realisation.

Howard's idea of setting up a formal trust was not possible because of the difficult financial position that the trustees might be placed in and because a joint stock enterprise was necessary to raise capital. The shareholders were to receive a cumulative dividend not exceeding five per cent per annum, while any balance of profit was to be applied to any purpose which the company or its directors might deem for the benefit of the town or its inhabitants. During the first year there were

(Above) Howard's first home in Letchworth at 2 Norton Way, cottages designed by Parker and Unwin in 1904. (Below) The 1904 conference of the Garden City Association at Letchworth. In the front row are seated, fifth from left, Ebenezer Howard next to Thomas Adams, secretary of the Association. Behind are, second from left, Raymond Unwin next to Barry Parker.

considerable financial difficulties as the shares which were without equity did not recommend themselves to investors, nor were they recommended as investments. Only those who had some interest in the project itself and could afford the limited, and by no means secure, return, took up shares. The enthusiasm of the board overcame what might have been insuperable obstacles and took up mortgages and loans to complete their transactions. By the end of the first year £100,692 had been raised while mortgages on the freeholds accounted for £83,934. It is evident that Howard was backed by men of more than ordinary nerve and resolution.

A PERSONAL LOSS

In his moment of triumph, fate struck Howard a cruel blow, for almost exactly a year after the October opening of the estate Mrs Howard died in their London home at Stamford Hill. She had lived just long enough to see the beginning of her husband's dream being realised; she had believed in the garden city and had done all she could to help and encourage him. Mrs Howard was buried in St Mary's churchyard, Letchworth, near the centre of the original estate. Whatever the extent of his personal grief, Howard had little chance to brood, being in the midst of his pioneer work, but if he did so there is little doubt that he drew comfort from the religious faith he and his wife had shared. The Mrs Howard Memorial Hall was built in her memory; it is fitting that it was the first public building to be built in the garden city, where it has served as a community meeting place ever since.

RAYMOND UNWIN AND BARRY PARKER

The leader of any new enterprise must choose his collaborators wisely if success is to be achieved. Howard did this in his choice of planners, Barry Parker and Raymond Unwin, who found in Letchworth a great opportunity to put into practice the ideas that had been forming in their minds for some time previously. They too had a great interest in the social problems caused by unrestrained urbanisation but their philosophies were based on backgrounds in which the liberal arts were strongly represented.

Born near Rotherham in 1863, Raymond Unwin was educated at Oxford and then became an apprentice engineer for

Staveley Coal and Iron Company, near Chesterfield. He began to show his interest in 'social' architecture during the early 1890s when he was concerned with building pithead baths and miners' cottages. In 1893 he married Ethel Parker, increasing his bond with her family by joining her brother, Barry, in an architectural partnership at Buxton in 1896. His brother-in-law was born at Chesterfield in 1867 and educated at Wesley College. He started the office in Buxton in the year before Unwin joined him.

Both young men wanted to express their convictions, which were greatly influenced by Ruskin and William Morris, in visual architecture. Their first undertaking outside private housing was New Earswick, near York, where Joseph Rowntree wished to establish an estate for his workers at the nearby cocoa factory. This was an important part of the social reform movement, more than a mere alleviation of poor housing and environmental conditions in industrial towns. It ranked as a forerunner of garden cities in that it paid attention deliberately to creating an environment which promoted health and happiness in its inhabitants. The planners were already in touch with the garden city movement and must have heard Howard declare at the Bournville Conference of 1901 that the plan in his book was merely a diagram and that he would not attempt to build a town anywhere without the best expert advice. In turn, Unwin made his views known in his remarks on 'The building of houses in the garden city'. He said: 'The successful setting out of such a work as a new city will only be accomplished by the frank acceptance of the natural conditions of the site; and, humbly bowing to these, by the fearless following out of some definite and orderly design based on them . . . such natural features should be taken as the keynote of the composition; but beyond this there must be no meandering in a false imitation of so-called natural lines.'

THE PLANNING

Probably because it was known that Unwin was especially sympathetic to Howard's views, the partners were invited to submit plans of a scheme for the estate at Letchworth in a competition sponsored by the Rowntree family. Plans were also submitted by W.R. Lethaby and Halsey Ricardo, and by Geoffrey Lucas and Sydney Cranfield. The Parker and Unwin

The quadrangle of Homesgarth, the Howards' second home in a co-operative housing venture. Howard was chairman of the company.

plan was accepted and, although intended only as a preliminary idea, it remained substantially unchanged. A large proportion of the features illustrated in Howard's diagrams appear in the town plan. These include the radiating roads from a civic centre, a factory district on the outskirts, and groups of houses around 'village-green' nuclei. Community life was to be promoted around these centres while those for whom this had no appeal were catered for in areas like the Broadway, the main axis of the design. Around these elements ran the agricultural or green belt containing the centuries-old villages of Norton, Willian and Letchworth. The whole layout had a freedom and looseness which banished any impression that it had been drawn with rulers and compasses, unlike so many nineteenth-century plans of Utopian aspect. The dwellings were set at a density of twelve or fewer houses to the acre and these were placed in positions which gave them pleasant prospects and sunny aspects. Ever ready to pay attention to any detail which would introduce beauty as well as design into the town, Parker believed that the destruction of a single tree should be avoided, unless absolutely necessary, and he used arboreal features to build up, or blot out, views. Use was made of the undulating nature of the terrain to provide vistas and prospects. By grouping numbers of houses together it was possible to have large gaps between the groups, thus providing views of gardens, countryside or buildings beyond.

The planners firmly believed that the kinds of architecture appearing in the garden city should be controlled. Building regulations specified the types of materials and the standards acceptable to the consultant architects. There is no doubt that some very strange structures managed to come into being, especially during the Cheap Cottages Exhibitions, but even these were in the spirit of the place. Parker, in particular, fought continually with the directors of the company over the erection of buildings in the town, but sites had to be let and would-be tenants often had their own ideas on what they required with little appreciation of the kind of standards required by him. The planning of Letchworth is bound to be open to some criticism, especially in the light of lessons learnt since 1903, but Parker and Unwin produced something that was unique and introduced to many fortunate people a kind of living they would never have thought possible.

CONSOLIDATION

Howard moved from London to Letchworth in 1905 and lived in a cottage built by Parker and Unwin at 2 Norton Way South, until 1912 when he moved to Homesgarth. During these years the town was growing, but this growth was accompanied by continual compromise due to the increasing demands of necessity, as opposed to ideals. The early years promoted a community spirit never to be repeated. Activities of all kinds ranged from Arbor Days, May Day festivities, amateur dramatics and poetry readings, to religious discussions and popular scientific lectures. Howard took part in many of these and was much in demand as a Thespian. He was President of the Arbor Day Celebrations in 1908 which were attended by Rudyard Kipling, and in the coronation procession of 1911 he carried the banner of the garden city.

Conferences and special visits from those interested in the movement became everyday occurrences; in August 1907

Howard was able to combine two of his main interests when five hundred members of the International Esperanto Congress visited Letchworth and he welcomed them with a speech in Esperanto. This interest had its root in Howard's strong feelings on the brotherhood of man, and he saw the language as a means of cutting across national barriers. He became President of the Letchworth Esperanto Society in 1911, attending the International Congress in Cracow in 1912 where he lectured on garden cities.

In 1908 Miss E.A. Hayward of Wilbury Road, Letchworth, became the second Mrs Howard; there were no children of this marriage. Among Howard's recreations was chess and he was considered to be a good player, probably another consequence of his ability to concentrate. A visitor to Norton Way South might also become involved by his hosts in a game of croquet on the lawn.

At this time the founder of the garden city was very much in evidence as he went about his various tasks. He attracted attention outside the garden city too, being granted a Civil List Pension in 1912 which, together with his director's fees from the company, was his main source of steady income. The Garden Cities and Town Planning Association gave a banquet in his honour on 19th March 1912 at the Holborn Restaurant with Earl Grey in the chair. Among those present were Lord Robert Cecil, Walter Crane, Rider Haggard, Cecil Harmsworth, Lord Northcliffe, Joseph Rowntree, George Bernard Shaw, besides several representatives of Germany, Belgium, the United States and Spain. Howard received a portrait of himself painted by Mr Spenser Pryse and a cheque which he declared would be devoted to the garden city movement. At this meeting the assembled company were told of the way in which the work of their guest of honour had become known all over the world, and that the Association was being asked to give advice to countries as far away as Australia. Such news must have been most welcome to 'the dreamer . . . who had enjoyed this rare distinction—that in the narrow space of twelve years he had been able to prove his dream to be true.'

At about this time the Howards moved their place of residence to Homesgarth, a venture of Letchworth Co-operative Houses Limited. It was a scheme which received Howard's support and interest, for it was a new idea and promoted a form

(Above) Howard, in uncharacteristic garb, taking part in the 1911 Coronation celebrations. (Left) Howard with his second wife at the May Day Festivals at Letchworth in 1913.

As an enthusiastic supporter of Esperanto, Howard attended a conference in Cracow in 1912 where he spoke, in Esperanto, on garden cities.

of community living which appealed to him. He was, in fact, chairman of the company. The scheme consisted of self-contained flats or small houses arranged around a quadrangle which had one partly open side. There was a central heating system and meals were provided in a dining room from a central kitchen. The private accommodation ranged from a flat with a single bedroom to one with three and service was provided; a similar scheme existed at Meadow Way Green.

A SECOND GARDEN CITY

In 1912 F.J. Osborn became secretary and manager of the Howard Cottage Society and began a lifetime's devotion to Howard's ideas and to Howard personally. Like his mentor he saw a great deal of Howard's work misunderstood and perverted but had the good fortune to see some of it put right. Howard himself had already become restless, and was eager to start another garden city. In 1910 he had proposed the founding of one as an international memorial to King Edward VII but this came to nothing. Not in the least discouraged, Howard fixed on the Welwyn area for the site which he showed to C.B. Purdom and F.J. Osborn in 1918. The story of the foundation of Welwyn Garden City is illustrative of the kind of man Howard was. He became obsessed with the venture, patiently working towards it, persisting in spite of all advice from his friends as to its commercial prospects. In May 1919 1,458 acres were purchased at the Panshanger sale, Howard having paid the ten per cent deposit which he had somehow managed to raise with the help of friends. All this was done on his own initiative, an action which some may have considered foolhardy; but events were to prove him right. In June letters were being sent out seeking subscribers, or loans at five per cent, and on 15th October the Second Garden City Limited was incorporated. The rest of the story is as well known as that of Letchworth.

Welwyn provided the garden city movement with an opportunity to make a fresh start which its leaders were eager to seize. Three written attempts were made to influence the government to recognise the part garden cities could play in its housing policy; these were *The Garden City After the War* by Purdom, *New Towns After the War* by Osborn and *A National Housing Policy* issued by the National Garden Cities Committee, but they failed to achieve any result. Howard's conduct in acting without waiting for government sponsorship was fully justified. Welwyn shows harmony of layout and architecture, its centre is truly impressive and its buildings and gardens are arranged to give maximum light and space. While there was no controlled shopping facility in Letchworth, it was possible to put into practice one of Howard's original ideas at Welwyn. This was in the form of the Welwyn Stores, a company in which the Garden City Company had a controlling interest, whose function was to provide maximum efficiency in the distribution of commodities in the town by controlling the shopping sites on the estate; Howard had a personal interest in the Stores. From 1921 until his death Ebenezer Howard was a Welwyn Garden citizen and lived at 5 Guessens Road.

During these years of public endeavour, invention had not been neglected; typewriters still loomed large in Howard's life. For some years he had become interested in making a silent shorthand machine and had completed his third prototype by 1924. This seemed to satisfy him and work had begun on the making of jigs and tools for production, as well as preparing

(Above) 5 Guessens Road, Howard's Welwyn home where he lived until his death in 1928. (Opposite) The general town plan of Welwyn Garden City drawn up by Louis de Soissons. The railway marked a north-south axis and is integral to the whole plan, unlike Letchworth.

textbooks for the machine. One of these has survived but there does not seem to be an extant copy of instructions. Howard seems to have had a great deal of faith in the commercial possibilities of the machine but shorthand typewriters had been on the market since the end of the previous century and a French model had demonstrated its efficiency by being in continual use for seventeen years since 1910. Such machines relied on phonetic characters, Howard's had eighty keys and worked on a code principle which had to be learned. It is amazing to think that such a matter was being undertaken not by a young hopeful, but by a man of public reputation in his mid-seventies!

Public life continued to make its demands and Howard was frequently asked to speak or preside at conferences and meetings, as well as being a magistrate. He was elected an

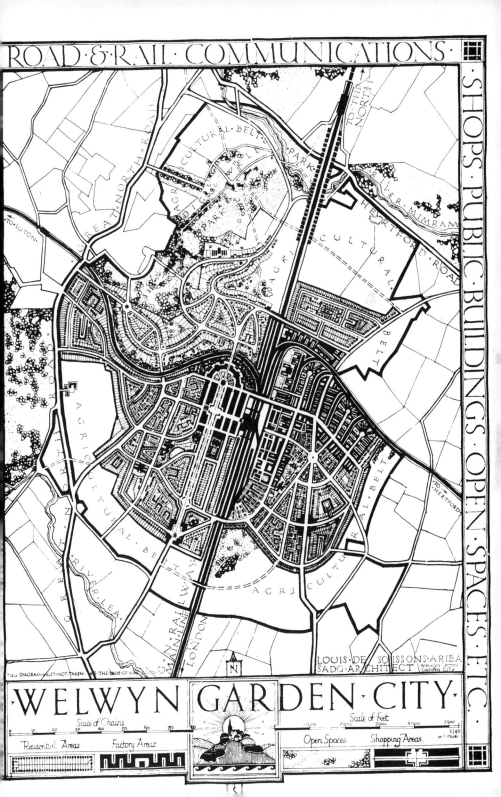

Howard's shorthand typewriter which he considered to be ready for manufacture shortly before his death.

Honorary Associate of the Royal Institute of British Architects, an Honorary Member of Leningrad Architects' Society, and was President of the International Federation of Town and Country Planning and Garden Cities.

In 1925 he made his last visit to the United States for a meeting of the Town Planning Institute where he received the honour due to him. The following year saw him engaged at Letchworth as chairman of a public conference on town planning at which the chief speaker was Neville Chamberlain. In the Civic Week celebrations Howard opened the proceedings and took part in an official reception held by the Urban District Council and the First Garden City Company.

HONOURING THE FOUNDER

Official recognition was so delayed as to be almost too late. In 1924 came an OBE and three years later a knighthood.

Thank you for shopping at Amazon.co.uk!

Invoice for
Your order of 12 February, 2014
Order ID 202-4854633-6814727
Invoice number D8tsNX3MN
Invoice date 12 February, 2014

Billing Address
Mark Capelin
5 Crabtree Lane
Lancing
Brighton, West Sussex BN15 9PF
United Kingdom

Shipping Address
Mark Capelin
5 Crabtree Lane
Lancing
Brighton, West Sussex BN15 9PF
United Kingdom

Qty.	Item		Our Price (excl. VAT)	VAT Rate	Total Price
1	**Ebanezer Howard (Shire Library)** Paperback, Eccardt, John. 0747811318 (** P-1-A38G21 **)		£5.91	0%	£5.91
	Shipping charges		£0.00		£0.00
	Subtotal (excl. VAT) 0%				£5.91
	Total VAT				£0.00
	Total				£5.91

Conversion rate - £1.00 : EUR 1,20

We've sent this portion of your order separately at no extra charge to give you the speediest
service possible. The other items in your order are shipping separately, and your total
postage and packing charges for this order will not exceed the amount we originally charged.

You can always check the status of your orders or change your account details from the 'Your Account' link at the top of each page on our site.

Thinking of returning an item? PLEASE USE OUR ON-LINE RETURNS SUPPORT CENTRE.

Our Returns Support Centre (www.amazon.co.uk/returns-support) will guide you through our Returns Policy and provide you with a printable personalised
return label. Please have your order number ready (you can find it next to your order summary, above). Our Returns Policy does not affect your statutory rights.

Amazon EU S.a.r.L, 5 Rue Plaetis, L-2338, Luxembourg
VAT number : GB727255821

Please note – this is not a returns address - for returns - please see above for details of our online returns centre

0/D2OGNn3ZN/-1 of 1-1//SMDA/econ-uk/7371153/0215-15:00/0212-16:21 Pack Type : A1

(Above) Parkway, Welwyn Garden City, is much closer to the grand boulevards of Howard's book than Letchworth's Broadway. (Below) Brockswood Lane, Welwyn Garden City, typical of a garden city street.

Bernard Shaw, on congratulating Howard, wrote that he 'should have a barony for his book, an earldom for Letchworth, and a dukedom for Welwyn', and referred to 'such an inadequate acknowledgement to his public services as a knighthood'. Howard most certainly did not care for the honour for his own sake but saw in it a recognition of the significance of the Garden City movement as a whole. A Complimentary Dinner was given in his honour on 4th February at which Neville Chamberlain, Minister of Health, proposed the toast to 'Sir Ebenezer Howard OBE' saying 'We meet tonight to do honour to a man with an idea.' People behaved as if Ebenezer Howard was a newly discovered phenomenon or an explorer returned from some distant land after many long years. At seventy-seven years of age with two garden cities to his credit, as well as a book which revolutionised the sociological thought of his day, Sir Ebenezer Howard must have wished that all this had happened at a time when he could have made better use of it for the furtherance of his movement, the dominating force in his life.

Throughout the years Howard had enjoyed very good health and had had few days of illness. However, in a letter written in June 1927 to J.W. Cole, he refers to 'a severe pain in my right leg which makes walking difficult and also sometimes prevents my concentrating my efforts'. In April 1928 he began to fail; on a visit to Letchworth he was so ill that he had to rest in the Peoples' House. He died at daybreak on May Day after spending the last two hours of his life unconscious, and was buried in Letchworth. Thus ended the career of a modest and remarkable man about whose personal affairs little more is known than is written above.

Ebenezer Howard was so much identified with his projects and ideas that his private existence became almost permanently public. The secret of his success was that he was cast in no other man's mould, like his more favoured contemporaries. His education was in the classroom of the outside world and, like the inventor he was, he made the tool of his mind as he wanted it. Being sent away to school at an early age made him self-reliant and self-sufficient while his great power of observation enabled him to see what was important and what was trivial. He was not interested in worldly wealth or success; his estate at his death was a mere £800, but his achievement was

Draft of a speech to be delivered during the General Strike, 1926, in Howard's handwriting.

so great that its effects are still being felt today. Howard was no 'personality' in today's sense of the word, he felt no desire to project himself but used himself to project his deeply held beliefs. He could be likened to a small source of great energy which quietly glows until it is activated for some significant purpose when it becomes unrecognisable in its intensity. Above the first chapter of *Garden Cities of Tomorrow* stands a quotation from Blake which, as much as anything, sums up the attitude of Howard to his chosen task, and he meant every word to apply literally:

'I will not cease from mental strife,
Nor shall my sword sleep in my hand,
Till we have built Jerusalem
In England's green and pleasant land.'

How much he succeeded is for all to see in his garden cities and in his written work which spread his ideas all over the world to the benefit of countless thousands, both past and yet to come.

Howardsgate, Welwyn Garden City, with the simple memorial on the left.

BIBLIOGRAPHY

The only attempt to write a biography of Ebenezer Howard was made in Dugald Macfadyen's *Sir Ebenezer Howard and The Town Planning Movement* (Manchester University Press, 1933). This is a first-hand account, often bordering on the adulatory, written in a style which makes it hard to get at the facts.

Exceedingly valuable are the contributions by F.J. Osborn: F.J. Osborn 'Sir Ebenezer Howard—The Evolution of His Ideas' in *The Town Planning Review* Vol.XXI No.3, October 1950, pages 221-235, and his Preface to *Garden Cities of Tomorrow,* (Faber and Faber Ltd., 1944). In the same book may be found an important essay on 'The Garden City Idea and Modern Planning' by Lewis Mumford.

W.A. Eden examines the origins of Howard's ideas in the light of other schemes current during the preparation of his book in a paper on 'Ebenezer Howard and the Garden City Movement' in *The Town Planning Review* Vol.XIX, 1947, pages 123-143. He traces the development of Howard's ideas with a thoroughness that seems to go beyond the facts that we know about the man himself. Lastly, he examines the garden city 'plan' as if it were a real town plan and had not been marked by its author: 'N.B. Diagram only. Plan cannot be drawn until site selected.'

The best history of the garden cities is contained in C.B. Purdom *The Building of Satellite Towns* (J.M. Dent & Sons, 1925), with a subsequent history of developments in Letchworth up to 1963 in *The Letchworth Achievement* (J.M. Dent & Sons, 1963). Much very useful information may be gleaned from reading *The Letters of Lewis Mumford and Frederick J. Osborn* (edited by Michael Hughes) (Adams and Dart, 1971), although some background knowledge of the subjects covered would add to its value. Numerous references to Ebenezer Howard are to be found in the majority of books dealing with the evolution of town planning. Of some interest is W.L. Creese *The Search for Environment* (Yale University Press, 1966).

THE PRINCIPAL EVENTS OF EBENEZER HOWARD'S LIFE

1850 Ebenezer Howard born
1851 *The Great Exhibition*
1865 Howard becomes a City clerk. *Abraham Lincoln assassinated*
1867 Howard teaches himself Pitman's shorthand. *Second Reform Bill*
1869 *Suez Canal opens*
1870 Howard becomes Dr Parker's secretary
1871 Howard sails for New York. The Chicago Fire
1872 Howard moves to Chicago and becomes a stenographer
1876 Howard returns to England and joins Gurney's
1878 *Edison produces electric light*
1879 Howard marries Elizabeth Ann Bills
1881 Howard becomes a land reformer after reading Henry George
1882 *Phoenix Park murders*
1884 *Third Reform Bill*
1885 *General Gordon slain at Khartoum*
1888 Howard reads Bellamy's *Looking Backward*
1895 *Marconi sends first wireless message*
1898 *Tomorrow: A Peaceful Path to Real Reform* published in October
1899 Formation of the Garden City Association. *Boer War begins*
1901 Conference at Bournville. *Death of Queen Victoria*
1902 Conference at Port Sunlight. Garden City Pioneer Company formed
1903 First Garden City registered and First Garden City opened at Letchworth. *Wright brothers make the first aeroplane flight*
1904 Mrs Howard dies. Building of Letchworth begins
1905 Howard moves to Letchworth
1906 *San Francisco earthquake*
1908 Howard marries Miss E.A. Hayward
1909 *Mass-production of Model T Ford. Old Age Pensions introduced in Britain*
1910 Howard proposes the founding of a garden city as a memorial to Edward VII

1911 *Parliament Act reduces power of Lords*
1912 Complimentary dinner by Garden Cities and Town Planning Association. Visit to Cracow
1914 *First World War breaks out*
1917 *Russian Revolution*
1918 *Germany defeated—Armistice signed*
1919 Howard buys part of the estate for Welwyn Garden City
1920 *First meeting of League of Nations*
1921 Howard moves to Welwyn Garden City
1924 Howard awarded OBE. The shorthand typewriter completed
1925 Visit to International Federation of Town Planning in USA
1927 Howard knighted. Complimentary dinner at Letchworth
1928 Howard dies at Welwyn on 1st May. *Votes for women in Britain*

The Howard Memorial in Howard Park, Letchworth, erected in 1930. The simple inscription reads 'Ebenezer Howard founded this town in 1903'.

INDEX
Page numbers in italic refer to illustrations